100 Minutes with God

*1 Minute Daily Devotions
of Timeless Inspiration*

By Susan Grant

ISBN: 9781671109162

"Victorian Pocket Watch Vector Graphics." Victorian Pocket Watch Vector Graphics, Openclipart, n.d., publicdomainvectors.org/en/free-clipart/Victorian-pocket-watch-vector-graphics/12574.html

Book Cover Design by Isabel Robalo - IsaDesign.net

Printed is the United States of America

Praise for
100 Minutes with God

"I have always started my day with some daily Scripture-based devotionals…I am grateful to add (these) to my morning reading list."
- Calvin Johnson

"I love your words." – H. Evenden

"Thank you. I needed this (devotion) today."
-E. Owens

"Beautiful thoughts and insights."
– A. Roach

For my grandfather, C.E. Long Jr.

Acknowledgements

Thank you to my husband, Randy, who has been and always will be my biggest fan and supporter. You have made this possible.

Many thanks also to my early email subscribers. Your comments and encouragement resulted in this book.

If you're interested in reading more of my work and being notified of new books, you can sign up for my newsletter at susan-grant.com.

If you have found this book helpful, please review it where you made your purchase.

Coming soon: 100 More Minutes with God

Table of Contents

Foreword

We live in a world that has the most technology and innovations in all of history. What used to take hours to cover a handful of miles you can now navigate in minutes. Our lives are busy, but we still need to make time for the things that are important.

100 Minutes with God makes it possible to connect with God each day. You can read each devotion in a minute, but its content provides you with material that you can contemplate throughout your day.

God longs to spend time with you. Why don't you join Him for a few minutes, today?

Minute 1

You Are Very Good

Genesis 1:31

On the 1st 5 days of creation, God looked at what He did and pronounced, "It is good," BUT on the 6th day, after God created people, He said, "It is Very good." God cares so much about you, He labeled you as 'very good.' God does care.

Notes:

Minute 2

God Changes Bad to Good

Genesis 50:20

Joseph realized that the bad things his brothers did to him; God used for good – the saving of lives in famine-stricken Egypt. God cares enough about you to take the worst life has to offer and make it good; He is in the re-creation business.

Notes:

Minute 3

I Will Help You.
I Promise

Exodus 4:13

Moses tried his way to help the enslaved Israelites in Egypt and failed. God tells him at the burning bush to do the job His way and promises 'I will help you speak and will teach you what to say'. God will always help His people when they need it.

Notes:

Minute 4

God's Love is Not Conditional

Exodus 34:6

Feel unaccepted, guilty, judged, criticized, or unlovable? There is hope! God's love is NOT conditional. He does not say, 'I will love you only if...' His love never runs out. God is "compassionate and gracious...slow to anger and abounding in love."

Notes:

Minute 5

You Are Blessed

Numbers 6:24-25

God cares enough to bless you. He promises it. He will "keep" you; building a protection around you. He will always be gracious; giving you only His best, whether you deserve it or not. He gives peace to His children.

Notes:

Minute 6

God Loves Everyone

Numbers 14:18

We live in an angry world, and this rubs off on us. These things do not affect God. He is slow to anger and abounding in love, for you. He is also slow to anger and abounding in love for those you may not see eye-to-eye with. God is love.

Notes:

Minute 7

God Does Not Lie

Numbers 23:19; Jeremiah 31:1

We've got half-truths, white lies, and fibs, but whatever you call them, they're all lies. God does not lie. He loves you with an everlasting love. No strings, no half-truths, no kidding.

Notes:

Minute 8

Fret or Relax;
It's Your Choice

Deuteronomy 4:35

God reminds Moses that he can see the works of God in his life if he would make the effort to reflect on them. Sometimes we get so caught up in the 'now' and fret when we could look back at God's faithfulness and relax.

Notes:

Minute 9

Follow the Leader

Deuteronomy 28:1-2

A wise teacher once told me, if you are ever on the fence about whether to give your life to God; follow His guidance and rules and see if it doesn't improve your life. Not sure? Try it; you have nothing to lose.

Notes:

Minute 10

God Will not Abandon You

Deuteronomy 31:8

If you know the pain of being abandoned, it's easy to believe that God may abandon you, too; He won't. It doesn't matter how imperfect, sinful, obnoxious or undeserving you are, He will NOT leave you.

Notes:

Minute 11

We Make Choices Daily

Joshua 24:15

Daily we have a slew of choices to make. What to wear, eat, say, do, and think. God tells us through Joshua that we must choose daily who we will serve; God or ourselves. To not choose is to choose; make an intentional choice today.

Notes:

Minute 12

God Wants to Spend Time with Me?

1 Samuel 15:22

We can get the idea that sacrificing for someone is more important than our relationship with that person. God wants our trust and obedience to come before anything else. He wants time with you.

Notes:

Minute 13

What God Sees

I Samuel 16:7

We spend so much time, money and energy on trying to make our bodies, something that is finite, look good or better. God says He looks at our hearts. Maybe we should spend more time working on how it looks.

Notes:

Minute 14

You Delight God!

2 Samuel 22:20

Did you have someone in your life, maybe a grandparent, whose face would light up when they saw you? How good it makes you feel inside. That's how God sees you. He will rescue you when needed because He delights in you.

Notes:

Minute 15

What's Your Motive?

1 Kings 8:39

It is easy to assume we know why others say and do what they do. We convince ourselves we have this ability, when in reality, only God does. We cannot possibly know the motives of others. God does, and He knows yours, too.

Notes:

Minute 16

He's on Your Side

1 Chronicles 28:20

If others picked on you when you were a child, perhaps you had a big brother to stand beside you. When the bully saw him, he left you alone. God is by our side, always. Nothing can get to you without Him allowing it for your good.

Notes:

Minute 17

God Knows Your Heart

2 Chronicles 6:30

Knowing the motives of others is tricky; we are often wrong. God knows our hearts. He knows when we attempt to do something good even if it backfires. He cares.

Notes:

Minute 18

God Is Not Hiding

2 Chronicles 15:4

Where is God? A common question people in distress ask. God promises that if you turn to Him in your distress, you WILL find Him. God is not hiding; He cares about you.

Notes:

Minute 19

On the Lookout

2 Chronicles 16:9

Many of us thought our parents had eyes in the back of their heads. They didn't, but they knew what we were up to. 2 Chronicles 16:9 tells us God is searching for hearts committed to Him. When He finds them, He promises to give us strength.

Notes:

Minute 20

Where to Focus Your Eyes

2 Chronicles 20:12

With so many things demanding our attention, it's hard to know where to focus. The Bible tells us to focus on God and His leadership. He will never mislead you; He is 100% dependable.

Notes:

Minute 21

Choose Your Battles & Who Fights Them

2 Chronicles 32:8

We hear we should choose our battles wisely and the good news is, we do not fight our spiritual battles alone. The Bible tells us that God will help and fight for us. Reach out and ask for His help to fight when a battle ensues.

Notes:

Minute 22

Finding the Good in the Bad

Job 2:10

It's easy to trust God when things go our way, but God's way sometimes includes the bad. Job understood this, accepting all things that came his way. God can take the bad in life and make it good if you'll let Him.

Notes:

Minute 23

I WILL See Him

Job 19:25-27

Sometimes I have difficulty praying to a God I cannot see. Be assured, He is there and the 'not seeing' is where faith comes in. God promises that one day, I WILL see Him, face to face. He will satisfy all my yearnings and it will be a joyful day.

Notes:

Minute 24

God is Great; God is Good

Psalm 13:6

A childhood prayer says, "God is great; God is good". Often, we do not struggle with the great part, but the good is sometimes hard to believe. All that comes our way, God makes good because He IS good. This is great.

Notes:

Minute 25

You are Delightful

Psalm 18:19

What are some things in your life that delight you? Dinner out, sunsets, a complement? The Psalmist tells us God delights in us. If we could see God's face, it would be lit up with delight when He sees us coming. Rejoice!

Notes:

Minute 26

Are My Words Pleasing to God?

Psalm 19:14

David was concerned that the words that came out of his mouth were pleasing to God. I wonder how many conversations would not take place if we remembered this. May our words be pleasing to God.

Notes:

Minute 27

God Knows Our Anguish

Psalm 31:11

Anguish, fortunately, doesn't come to most of us often. When it does, others may know of its presence in our lives but only in a limited way. God knows the depth of our anguish and will love us through it. God's love comes at the right time!

Notes:

Minute 28

God Cares About Our Broken Hearts

Psalm 34:18; John 11:35

Sometimes we mistake the fact that because God allows hurtful things to happen to us, it means He does not care about our broken hearts. He cares deeply and even weeps over it. He saves those crushed in spirit.

Notes:

Minute 29

Being Still With God

Psalm 46:10

There are very few places these days that are quiet and still. It sometimes seems that people are trying to avoid it but in being still, we can hear God speak to us through His word and in our hearts. I challenge you to be still!

Notes:

Minute 30

The Voice of a Child

Psalm 55:16-17

When your child calls out to you in the middle of the night, you jump up, eager to help and protect. God also hears our cries, morning, noon and night; eager to help and protect. Cry out to Him because He cares about you.

Notes:

Minute 31

Want Some Rest?

I Corinthians 10:13

Do you find yourself in need of true rest and quiet? It comes from God alone because we can trust that He will take even the bad and make it good. He is in control. He will not give you more than you can handle.

Notes:

Minute 32

God Forgives & Forgets

Psalm 103:12

It is not helpful when someone tells us to forgive and forget. We cannot do this on demand. God forgives and forgets because He can. When we ask for forgiveness, He graciously gives it, remembering it no more.

Notes:

Minute 33

Our Days are Numbered

Psalm 90:12; 2 Corinthians 5:8

Our days are numbered. Does this sound scary?
If we are God's children, being aware of this
temporal life is important; it helps us set our
priorities. Besides, "to be absent from the body is
to be present with the Lord."

Notes:

Minute 34

I Rest My Case

Psalm 91:1

Rest is desirable, mentally, emotionally, and spiritually. Psalm 91:1 tells us that rest is already available to those who commune with God. The company you keep can provide the rest you so desperately crave. Choose your company wisely.

Notes:

Minute 35

Love God; Hate Evil

Psalm 97:10

There's just something that is intriguing about evil: Satan, the underworld, and mass murders, for example. The Psalmist admonishes us to love God and hate evil. Sometimes we need to place the evil beside the ultimate good in order to realize how bad evil is.

Notes:

Minute 36

The Gift of Love & Compassion

Psalm 103:4

We often see anger, judgment, and hostility in others these days. Psalm 103 tells us that God crowns us with love and compassion. If God, who knows everything about us, is compassionate toward us, we should freely give this gift to others.

Notes:

Minute 37

You Are Precious

Psalm 116:15

Death, and all that leads up to it, is hard to deal with. When a loved one dies, we yearn for their presence once again. Psalm 116 tells us that God is on the other end of this yearning. He loves it when His children leave this world and join Him. You are precious to Him.

Notes:

Minute 38

Let Go of Garbage

Psalm 119:37; Mark 8:36

Sometimes we hold on to things that are worthless and even time-bound. We need wisdom and guidance to discern between valuable and garbage. Don't gain the world but lose your soul.

Notes:

Minute 39

God Promises to Help
If You Ask

Psalm 121:1-2

Help! A single word that carries a strong message. Trying to navigate this life on our own is difficult. We need help and guidance. God has it ready for you, if you'll just ask Him. Why not ask? What have you got to lose?

Notes:

Minute 40

The Value of Forgiveness

Deuteronomy 32:35

It's easy to keep a mental record of wrongs we have endured by others. What's hard is to forgive. Forgiving is letting go of the need for revenge and allowing God to even the score.

Notes:

Minute 41

A Guard Over My Mouth

Psalm 141:3

Ever said something and then regretted it? It's easy to let our words fly out, but we should weigh them first. The Psalmist asked God to set a guard over his mouth. The world would be a better place if we were more careful with our words.

Notes:

Minute 42

The Big Picture

Proverbs 3:5-6

In a crowded room, all you can see is what's right in front of you. Sometimes we see our lives this way. God sees the big picture and we need to trust Him. This is hard to do when all we see is what's in front of us. Look up!

Notes:

Minute 43

Get to Know God

Proverbs 9:10

It is foolish to trust someone you don't know.
Getting to know someone helps you decide if
they are trustworthy. When it comes to God,
do not rely on others' views of who He is.
You get to know God by studying the Bible.
God is trustworthy.

Notes:

Minute 44

Do Not Worry

Proverbs 12:25; Matthew 6:34

Worry is bad for your body, mind, and spirit. Jesus went further to say not to worry about tomorrow; He will provide what you need for today. Worrying is often about something we can't control but God *is* in control.

Notes:

Minute 45

The Company You Keep

Proverbs 13:20

Many times, parents urge their teens to choose their friends wisely because they are so influenced by their peers. As adults, we still need to heed this advice, in fact, the Bible says this is wise. Others do influence us.

Notes:

Minute 46

Anger Management

Proverbs 15:1

We live in an angry world. Many seem to have a hair-trigger temper. The Bible tells us the best response to this is to be calm. Our "gentle answer" can turn a volatile situation around.

Notes:

Minute 47

The Myth of "Sticks & Stones"

Proverbs 15:4

The saying of 'sticks and stones' not hurting is preposterous. Proverbs says words can crush spirits. The good news is, our words can also bring healing. What type of words will we use today?

Notes:

Minute 48

Unanswered Prayers Can be a Blessing

Proverbs 16:9

How many times have we pleaded with God for something we were sure we needed? The Bible tells us we can plan all we want, but God determines our steps. These steps might lead to difficulties, but they will always be for our good!

Notes:

Minute 49

God Tests Our Hearts

Matthew 7:1; Proverbs 17:3

Many people tell us not to judge the motives of others, but, the hard news is, God judges our motives (heart). He is looking for its purity as one does with silver and gold. God knows that a pure heart is best for us.

Notes:

Minute 50

Others' Attitudes Affect Ours

Proverbs 17:22

Parents tell their children to choose their friends wisely, but adults need to choose wisely, too. Others' attitudes rub off on us. Some people we have to be around so we need to be watchful that we don't adopt their negativity.

Notes:

Minute 51

Winners & Losers

Ecclesiastes 9:11; Ecclesiastes 12:13

People sometimes label a person successful by different standards than God's. The fastest or strongest isn't always the best. Respecting God enough to keep His commands is the goal toward success in God's eyes.

Notes:

Minute 52

Mercy & Grace

Isaiah 1:18

Forgiveness is a misunderstood thing. It involves mercy and grace. Mercy is not getting something you deserve (punishment); grace is getting something you don't deserve (forgiveness). God washes our sins away if you ask Him to; mercy and grace.

Notes:

Minute 53

Standing Firm

Isaiah 7:9

Standing firm for something is a choice; so is not standing firm. Isaiah tells us that if we don't stand for our faith, we communicate that God is not important to us. What and who are you standing for?

Notes:

Minute 54

The Prince of Peace

Isaiah 9:6

We are now living in a world far from peaceful. I wonder if Amazon would crash if it offered peace for sale. Everyone wants it, but only God provides it. It's free. Ask Him for it!

Notes:

Minute 55

Who Told You?

Genesis 3:11; John 3:16

If you think you're worthless, it would be good to consider the question God asked Adam and Eve in the garden: "Who told you?" All our true value comes from God. The price paid for anything determines its value. Jesus died for you, so you are valuable.

Notes:

Minute 56

Forever & Ever

Isaiah 11:5

Loyalties and commitments don't always mean they're good for a lifetime. When God, in His faithfulness to us, says, "I Do," it means forever.

Notes:

Minute 57

Be Strong (Dependently)

Isaiah 12:2

In difficulty, we often hear the words, "Be Strong!" The problem is that we're human and being strong can be a burden too heavy to bear. God tells us we can be strong when we depend on Him. I'm strong because He is.

Notes:

Minute 58

Mind Control

Isaiah 26:3

Exercising and disciplining our thoughts takes a lot of energy. Isaiah tells us that perfect peace can be yours as long as your mind is steadfast (supported) on God. Our thoughts support our feelings, which can brings peace.

Notes:

Minute 59

God Loves Being Gracious to You

Isaiah 30:18

I have read that people often view God through the lens of what they experienced with their earthly fathers. For some, this is good; others, not. Isaiah tells us God LONGS to be compassionate with you. He loves you!

Notes:

Minute 60

Comfort & Joy

Isaiah 40:1

At Christmas, you hear the line, "O tidings of comfort and joy." There is a great yearning in these words. Isaiah laments, "Comfort, comfort (God's) people." God is the Comforter; go to Him and curl up on His lap.

Notes:

Minute 61

The Grass & Flowers

Isaiah 40:6-7

So much of what concerns us is temporary, like grass and flowers. These die when winter comes and Isaiah draws our attention to it as a reminder. A look from this perspective helps us deal with the temporary difficulties of life.

Notes:

Minute 62

Softly & Tenderly

Isaiah 40:11

Feeling unimportant and unloved? Isaiah tells us that God gathers us to Him like a shepherd gently gathers a little lamb and holds it close. God Almighty loves to hold us close. You ARE important and loved.

Notes:

Minute 63

Fear of Rejection

Isaiah 41:9

Many psychologists say rejection is the number one fear people have. It hurts when someone rejects you. Isaiah tells us God, Who knows everything about us, has chosen us and not rejected us. We have no fear of rejection from Him.

Notes:

Minute 64

Feeling Unimportant?

Isaiah 43:1

There are so many people needing things and asking God for them. This thought can make you feel lost in the crowd of other seekers. Isaiah says that God knows you by name and calls you to be His. Now, *that* makes you important and a priority to God. Rejoice!

Notes:

Minute 65

The Light on Darkness

Isaiah 45:3

Dark times will come our way. There's no getting around it. BUT Isaiah tells us there is a great treasure in the darkness of our lives. Faith digs for these treasures that God supplies. Where's your shovel?

Notes:

Minute 66

The Wonderful or the Good?

Isaiah 58:11

We sometimes settle for good when God wants to give us wonderful. Isaiah tells of God's satisfaction, strength, and water from a spring that doesn't go dry. Don't turn down thirst-quenching water for a quick drink that must be repeated.

Notes:

Minute 67

Who is Dependable?

Jeremiah 17:5-8

Who do you depend on to make your day good? Who do you turn to to help you deal with stress? People are limited and fallible so they will disappoint you. Jeremiah tells us God is dependable. He will keep you rooted and strong. Trust Him.

Notes:

Minute 68

Don't Mess with Me!

Jeremiah 20:11

Jeremiah tells us that God is our mighty
Warrior; He will let no one mess with us unless
it will produce a better good. Feel alone? God
has your back better than any human! Because
God is our warrior, we can face what's ahead.

Notes:

Minute 69

What is Your Source?

Jeremiah 23:16

Many people attribute words and thoughts to God, when, in fact, they are contrary to Who He is. When someone speaks on God's behalf, challenge it. Ask, what is your source? Don't be passive and accept it. Truth will hold up to any challenge.

Notes:

Minute 70

What Seems vs. What Is?

Jeremiah 29:11

Looking at a brown puzzle piece, it's easy to conclude that the picture is of mud. In reality, the picture is a mountain range, regal & majestic. God's plans for you may seem like mud, but they are always part of the beautiful good picture. Have hope!

Notes:

Minute 71

Love Beyond the Grave

Jeremiah 31:3

Perfect love is powerful because it has a level playing field. You don't move up the love ladder by actions, words, money, or status. God's love is yours just because you are you. This love is not conditional and it's eternal.

Notes:

Minute 72

Forgive & Forget?

Jeremiah 31:34

As Christians, God commands us to forgive. This difficult task is even harder because we cannot forget on demand. God does not forgive on demand either; He forgives by choice and remembers our sin no more. Rejoice!

Notes:

Minute 73

Life is Hard

Jeremiah 32:17

Some days I come home, barely able to put
one foot in front of the other. This is true
spiritually, too. Life is hard; it's a fact but for God,
NOTHING is too hard. Lean on Him; He longs
to hold you up.

Notes:

Minute 74

No Call Waiting

Jeremiah 33:3

People are so busy these days, I am reluctant to ask for any additional time from them. God is never too busy. He asks you to call on Him and He always answers. He yearns to share time with you.

Notes:

Minute 75

Compassion,
Each Day

Lamentations 3:22-23

The act of compassion (and, yes, it is a verb) is scarce these days. It is a choice to see with God's eyes rather than our judgmental ones. God's love and compassion for us and others are new every morning. We should give to others what we receive from God.

Notes:

Minute 76

No Pleasure
in Our Pain

Ezekiel 18:32

For some, it is satisfying to see someone who has wronged you be given their 'just deserts.' God NEVER takes pleasures in our pain or death; even when we brought it on ourselves. He loves us and wants us to do the right things.

Notes:

Minute 77

Redemption!
An Expensive Word

Ezekiel 33:11; 2 John 3:16

God is in the redemption business. He wants
to redeem all people, no matter what they have
done. It's His gift through His Son. No gift is
yours until you accept it. Thank God for His
redemption; it cost Him Jesus' life.

Notes:

Minute 78

I'm Not Who I Was

Ezekiel 36:26; John 3:16; Revelation 20:15

Looking back on my life, I cringe. Not for long

when I remind myself that I'm not who I was.

God has given me a new heart and a new spirit.

He's given them to you, too, if your name is in the

Book of Life. Are you on the books?

Notes:

Minute 79

The Gift of Mercy

Daniel 9:18

Mercy is not getting a punishment we deserve.
Daniel reminds us we can come to God with
our requests not because of our righteousness
(you know, those filthy rags?) but because of His
mercy. It's a gift, not an obligation.

Notes:

Minute 80

Apologies Always Accepted

Joel 2:13

When we wrong another, an apology is the starting point of making it right. God longs for us to come to Him when we've wronged Him; He will always accept our apology. Go to Him; He is gracious and compassionate.

Notes:

Minute 81

Act, Love & Walk

Micah 6:8

Ever wonder specifically what God wants you to do? It's simple: Act justly (as God sees justice; not your idea of it); love mercy (not treating others as they deserve when they have wronged you); and walk humbly (I am a sinner, saved by grace) with God. Act, love and walk.

Notes:

Minute 82

What God Sees

Micah 7:19

God promises us that in his compassion and love, He'll hurl our sins into the sea. Why do we go diving, trying to bring them back up? God has buried them; drowned them at sea. Leave them there.

Notes:

Minute 83

Is God Good?

Nahum 1:7

When we ask, 'why God?' we are often thinking, is God good? God is our refuge when difficulties come our way. He IS good, even if 'good' hurts in the immediate. He cares about you, always.

Notes:

Minute 84

How Long, O Lord?

Habakkuk 1:2-3, 5; Revelation 22:20

As I see and hear of murder, abuse, natural disasters, degrading words and more, it makes me lament Habakkuk's prayer: "How Long, O Lord? When will You act?" God's reply, "Watch and see". John said it best, "Come, Lord Jesus."

Notes:

Minute 85

Faith is Not a Feeling

Habakkuk 2:4

Some think faith is a feeling, but it's not. It is the mental assurance that the object of your faith will keep his or her word. You can relax because they are dependable. Only God can always keep His promises. Stand on this, even when your feelings say otherwise.

Notes:

Minute 86

Looks Can Be Deceiving

Habakkuk 3:17-19

Life can seem out of control and can give the feeling of hopelessness, but looks and feelings can be deceiving. No matter how bad it looks and feels, God gives strength. He urges us to do the difficult things because we are not doing them on our own power. It's all about Him.

Notes:

Minute 87

Being Rocked by God

Zephaniah 3:17

There are times, as an adult, when I long for God to hold and rock me when difficulties overwhelm my spirit. Coming to God with this need delights Him. He promises to quiet me with the assurance of His love. He rejoices when I come to Him. He feels this way with you, too. Go to Him.

Notes:

Minute 88

Human Frailty

Zechariah 4:6

God asked many in the Bible to do impossible things. How cruel would it be if God required something we cannot do without giving us the strength of His spirit to do them? When God gives us tasks, He always gives the means to do them.

Notes:

Minute 89

Skeletons in Jesus' Closet

Matthew 1

Most families have skeletons in their closets. Jesus' earthy family did, too. They included Tamar's rape; Rahab the prostitute, murdered Uriah's wife, to name a few. It is vital to note that God covered all involved in these 'secrets' with grace and forgiveness. The good news is, you are, too!

Notes:

Minute 90

Are You Hungry?

Matthew 5:6

In Jesus' day, many believed God blessed the most godly with power and wealth. Jesus stated otherwise. The book of Matthew tells us that the blessed are those who are hungry for righteousness (right-ness); these seekers and adopters receive God's blessings.

Notes:

Minute 91

I Am a Murderer

Matthew 5:22

Have I ever been angry at someone? Yes. I am guilty of murder. Why? Because anger is the seed of the action. Though it sidesteps legal consequences, Jesus said the thought is as bad as the deed. Our feelings and treatment of others grow from our thoughts.

Notes:

Minute 92

Battling 21st Century Enemies

Matthew 5:44

Trash-talking our enemies or those who think differently rarely results in good things. The book of Matthew says this is not okay. We are to love and pray for our enemies. Being hateful justifies many of their behaviors. Instead, battle with love and prayer. It's what God requires and it will set a better example for those around us.

Notes:

Minute 93

Instant vs. Eternal; Little vs. Huge

Matthew 6:2-3

If you ask many teens if he or she wants an aging car now versus waiting two years for a brand-new car, many would choose the now. Jesus said in Matthew that we can earn praise now from man for our giving or give secretly, and God will reward you later. Choose: Now or later.

Notes:

Minute 94

Treasure Maps

Matthew 6:21

We treasure many things, including some we cannot buy. We treasure family, friends, pets, jobs, status, or reputations. Jesus reminds us that our hearts or priorities reflect what we treasure. What does your treasure map reveal?

Notes:

Minute 95

Easier Said Than Done

Matthew 6:25

Jesus said not to worry, but that's difficult because worry is fear in disguise and fear can be hard to deal with. Some dress up worry as planning; others don't give it a second thought. If we spend our time getting to know God, we'd realize that He has all these things under His control. Don't worry!

Notes:

Minute 96

Yardsticks & Planks

Matthew 7:1-6

"Judge not" are two words many quote from
the Bible but few know this judging in context
means, to determine value. Jesus said measure
your thoughts and actions, removing your planks
before you worry about someone else's sawdust.
We are not always good value assessors.

Notes:

Minute 97

I Am the Greatest

Matthew 20:26-28

The most powerful is not the one with the biggest weapons, strongest muscles or loudest mouth. Jesus said the greatest is the servant; the one who loves others. Love changes others, including the one who gives it away.

Notes:

Minute 98

Hard Words in the Perfect Package

Mark 10:21; I Corinthians 13:13

Sometimes we must address difficult things. The way we package our words gives them power. If they're spewed out in anger, others reject this package. Jesus spoke such words, packaging them in love because "the greatest of these is love".

Notes:

Minute 99

The Little Things Count

Luke 16:10

If you want to discern what someone is made of, watch how they handle the little everyday things. If they are faithful, kind and just with these things, you can trust them to be the same way with the big things of life. How do you handle the little things?

Notes:

Minute 100

Requests vs. Relationship

Luke 18:1-8

Ever wonder if God tires of you asking Him the same things over and over? He does not. He eagerly wants to hear from you because He wants a relationship with you. The God of all the universe wants to spend time with you!

Notes:

About the Author

Susan Grant is a graduate of Columbia International University. She taught Bible history in the public schools of North Carolina for eighteen years and was instrumental in growing the program from one full-time teacher to three. Susan now teaches language arts and lives with her husband on the beautiful coast of Maine. When she's not teaching or writing, Susan enjoys reading, sewing and playing with her dachshund, Boone.

You can read more of Susan's writing at susan-grant.com